I0490648

Mastering Linux Administration: Essential Skills and Best Practices

By

Dr Issa Ngoie

CHAPTERS OVERVIEW

1. **Introduction to Linux Administration**: This chapter would cover the basics of Linux administration, including an overview of different Linux distributions, the Linux file system, and common administrative tasks.

2. **Essential Linux Administration Skills:** This chapter would dive deeper into the essential skills needed to be a successful Linux administrator, such as configuring network interfaces, managing user accounts, and setting up SSH access.

3. **Best Practices for Linux Administration**: In this chapter, you would cover some of the best practices that Linux administrators should follow, such as implementing backups and disaster recovery plans, keeping software up-to-date, and monitoring system performance.

4. **Advanced Linux Administration**: This chapter would explore some of the more advanced topics in Linux administration, such as kernel tuning, configuring security settings, and managing services and daemons.

5. **Troubleshooting Linux Systems**: The final chapter would focus on troubleshooting common issues that can arise when administering Linux systems, such as identifying and fixing network connectivity problems, resolving hardware and software issues, and debugging performance problems.

CONTENTS

CHAPTERS OVERVIEW 2

HISTORY OF LINUX 6

BEFORE LINUX 7

how to become a linux administrator? 8

linux torvald...10

BEST LINUX CERTIFCATIONS AND LINKS....................................12

Chapter 1: Introduction to Linux Administration.....................14

Real-world scenarios of common Linux administrative tasks:...24

Introduction to Linux glossary 30

An Introduction to Linux Basics 32

    Prerequisites..33

    The Terminal 33

The Filesystem Hierarchy Standard 35

Navigation 36

File Manipulation 40

CHAPTER 2: ESSENTIAL LINUX ADMINISTRATION SKILLS 47

linux administration real world scenario 49

Chapter 3 : Best Practices for Linux Administration 61

Chapter 4 : Advanced Linux Administration.............................62

Chapter 5: Troubleshooting Linux Systems 66

Linux Tools for Network Troubleshooting................................72

    ping...72

    ifconfig..73

    traceroute..74

Linux Boot Issue Troubleshooting: An Example 75

Linux File System Troubleshooting: An Example 77

Useful Linux Commands for System Administrators 79

1. Uptime Command 79

2. W Command 80

Available Options 80

3. Users Command...80

4. Who Command 81

5. Whoami Command 82

6. ls Command...82

7. Crontab Command 83

8. Less Command...83

9. More Command 84

10. CP Command...84

11. MV Command..85

12. Cat Command..85

13. cd command (change directory)...........................85

14. pwd command (print working directory) 85

15. Sort command 86

16. VI Command...86

17. SSH Command (Secure Shell) 86

18. Ftp or sftp Command...87

19. Systemctl Command...87

20. Free command..88

21. Top Command 89

22. Tar Command 90

23. Grep Command..90

24. Find Command 90

25. lsof Command...91

26. last command 92

27. ps command...93

28. kill command...93

29. rm command...94

30. mkdir command example. 94

linux administartion glossary................................95

HISTORY OF LINUX

Linux is a free and open-source operating system that was first developed by Linus Torvalds in 1991. Torvalds was a computer science student at the University of Helsinki in Finland, and he created Linux as a personal project.

At the time, most computer operating systems were proprietary, meaning they were developed and owned by specific companies. Torvalds wanted to create an operating system that was freely available to anyone who wanted to use it and contribute to its development.

Linux was originally based on another open-source operating system called MINIX, which was developed by Andrew S. Tanenbaum. Torvalds used MINIX as a starting point and began developing his own operating system, which he called Linux.

The early versions of Linux were command-line based and did not have a graphical user interface. However, as the operating system gained popularity, developers began creating graphical user interfaces and other tools to make it easier to use.

Linux quickly gained a following among developers and technology enthusiasts, and it began to be used in a wide range of applications, from servers to supercomputers. Today, Linux is used by millions of people around the world, and it is the backbone of many of the world's largest websites and IT infrastructures.

Linux has also spawned many other open-source projects, such as the Apache web server, the MySQL database system, and the Python programming language. These tools have become essential parts of the modern technology stack, and they continue to evolve and improve thanks to the contributions of the open-source community.

BEFORE LINUX

Before the creation of **Linux in 1991**, computer operating systems were primarily proprietary, meaning they were owned and controlled by private companies. The most popular operating system at the time was Microsoft's MS-DOS, which was a command-line interface that required users to type in specific commands to execute tasks.

Unix, which was created in the **1970s**, was an early operating system that was widely used in academic and research settings. However, it was expensive and not widely accessible to the general public.

In the late 1980s, Richard Stallman and the Free Software Foundation created the GNU Project, which aimed to develop a completely free and open-source operating system. While the GNU Project made significant progress in developing software, they were missing a crucial component: the kernel.

This is where **Linus Torvalds** comes in. In 1991, Torvalds, a student at the University of Helsinki, released the first version of the Linux kernel, which was open-source and freely available. Over time, developers around the world contributed to the development of the Linux operating system, which became one of the most widely used operating systems in the world, powering everything from smartphones to supercomputers.

how to become a linux administrator?

To become a Linux administrator, you will need to develop a combination of technical skills and knowledge, as well as practical experience working with Linux systems. Here are some steps you can take to become a Linux administrator:

1. **Develop a strong foundation in Linux**: Start by learning the basics of Linux, such as the command line interface, file system structure, and common commands. There are many free online resources available, including tutorials, videos, and forums.
2. **Get hands-on experience**: Set up a Linux environment on your own computer or use a virtual machine, and practice performing common administrative tasks, such as user management, system updates, and package installation.

3. **Get certified**: Consider obtaining a certification in Linux administration, such as the CompTIA Linux+ or the Red Hat Certified System Administrator (RHCSA) certification. These certifications can help demonstrate your skills and knowledge to potential employers.

4. **Gain practical experience**: Look for opportunities to gain practical experience with Linux systems, such as internships, volunteer work, or entry-level jobs. This can help you develop your skills and knowledge and build a portfolio of work that can showcase your abilities.

5. **Stay up-to-date with the latest technology**: Keep up with the latest trends and developments in Linux administration, and continue to develop your skills and knowledge by attending training courses, workshops, and conferences.

Becoming a Linux administrator requires a combination of technical skills, practical experience, and a passion for learning and staying up-to-date with the latest technology. With dedication and hard work, you can develop the skills and knowledge needed to succeed in this exciting and rewarding field.

linux torvald

Linus Torvalds is the creator of the Linux operating system. He started developing Linux in 1991 as a student at the University of Helsinki in Finland. Originally, Linux was just a hobby project, but it quickly gained popularity and became one of the most widely used operating systems in the world, powering everything from servers and supercomputers to smartphones and embedded devices.

Linus Torvalds is still involved in the development of Linux today, serving as the maintainer of the Linux kernel, which is the core component of the operating system. He continues to work on new features and improvements for the kernel, collaborating with a large community of developers and contributors from around the world. In recognition of his contributions to the field of computer science, Linus Torvalds has received numerous awards and honors, including the Millennium Technology Prize in 2012 and the IEEE Computer Society Computer Pioneer Award in 2014.

how to get jobs as linux administration ?

Here are some tips for getting a job as a Linux administrator:

1. **Develop your skills**: Start by learning and mastering the essential skills required for Linux

administration, such as system installation and configuration, shell scripting, networking, security, and troubleshooting. You can take online courses, read books and articles, and practice on your own systems or virtual machines.

2. **Gain experience**: Look for opportunities to gain hands-on experience in Linux administration. You can participate in open-source projects, contribute to online forums and communities, or volunteer for local non-profit organizations that use Linux. You can also set up your own systems and networks at home or on a cloud platform like AWS or Azure.

3. **Build a portfolio**: Create a portfolio of your work and accomplishments in Linux administration. This can include your own projects, contributions to open-source projects, certifications, and examples of problems you have solved.

4. **Network**: Connect with other Linux professionals and organizations by attending conferences, meetups, and online forums. You can also join professional associations like the Linux Professional Institute (LPI) or the Linux Foundation.

5. **Look for job opportunities**: Search for Linux administration jobs on job boards, company websites, and professional associations. You can also reach out to companies that use Linux and

inquire about job openings or opportunities for contract work.

6. **Prepare for interviews**: Be ready to discuss your experience, skills, and achievements in Linux administration during job interviews. Be prepared to answer technical questions, demonstrate your problem-solving abilities, and show your enthusiasm for the field.

Remember that Linux administration is a constantly evolving field, so stay up to date with the latest technologies and trends. This will help you stand out from other candidates and demonstrate your commitment to the profession.

BEST LINUX CERTIFCATIONS AND LINKS

Here are some of the best Linux certifications available, along with links to their respective websites:

1. **Red Hat Certified System Administrator (RHCSA):** This certification is designed to test and validate the skills and knowledge required to work as a Linux system administrator. It is widely recognized in the industry and can help open doors to job opportunities. **https://www.redhat.com/en/services/certification/rhcsa**

2. **Linux Professional Institute Certification (LPIC):** The LPIC certification is a vendor-neutral

certification program that tests for proficiency in Linux administration. The certification is broken into three levels of expertise, ranging from basic to advanced skills. **https://www.lpi.org/**

3. **CompTIA Linux+ Certification**: This certification is designed to test and validate the skills and knowledge required to work as a Linux system administrator. It covers both the Linux command line and graphical interface, and is recognized by many employers. **https://www.comptia.org/certifications/linux**

4. **SUSE Certified Administrator (SCA):** This certification is designed to test and validate the skills and knowledge required to work with SUSE Linux Enterprise Server. It covers installation, configuration, and administration of SUSE Linux. **https://www.suse.com/training/certification/sca/**

5. **Oracle Linux Certifications**: Oracle offers several Linux certifications, including the Oracle Certified Professional, Oracle Linux Administrator certification, and the Oracle Certified Expert, Oracle Linux 6 System Administrator certification. These certifications demonstrate proficiency in Oracle Linux administration. **https://education.oracle.com/linux**

These certifications can help you demonstrate your skills and knowledge to potential employers and advance your career in Linux administration.

Chapter 1: Introduction to Linux Administration

what is systems administration ?

system vs administartion

The terms "system" and "administration" are related but refer to different things in the context of computer technology.

A system refers to a collection of hardware, software, and data that work together to perform a specific task or set of tasks. A computer system, for example, includes a CPU, memory, storage devices, input/output devices, an operating system, and various applications and utilities.

Administration, on the other hand, refers to the management and maintenance of computer systems and networks. This includes tasks such as installing and configuring hardware and software, monitoring system performance, ensuring security and data backups, and troubleshooting system issues.

In other words, system refers to the technical components that make up a computer system, while administration refers to the human activity of managing and maintaining those components.

In summary, while a computer system is the technical infrastructure that supports computing, administration involves the human activities and processes involved in managing and maintaining that system.

Systems administration is the process of managing and maintaining computer systems and networks. This includes tasks such as installing and configuring hardware and software, monitoring system performance, ensuring security and data backups, and troubleshooting system issues. Systems administrators are responsible for ensuring that the computer systems and networks are running smoothly and efficiently, with minimal downtime and interruptions. They need to have a good understanding of computer hardware, software, and networking technologies, as well as knowledge of operating systems and applications used in their organizations. They also need to be familiar with various tools and utilities used for system administration, such as network monitoring software, backup and recovery tools, and diagnostic tools. Systems administration is a critical function in any organization that relies on computer systems and networks, and skilled systems administrators are in high demand in today's technology-driven world.

Linux administration is the process of managing and maintaining a Linux-based operating system. Linux is an open-source operating system that is widely used in servers, supercomputers, and mobile devices. Linux administration involves tasks such as installing and configuring the operating system, managing user accounts and permissions, updating and patching the system, managing software packages, configuring system services, monitoring system performance, and troubleshooting system issues. Linux administrators need to have a good understanding of the Linux command line interface, file system, network configuration, and security. They also need to be familiar with various tools and utilities used for system administration, such as package managers, log files, and diagnostic tools. With the growing popularity of Linux, there is a high demand for skilled Linux administrators who can manage and maintain Linux-based systems efficiently and effectively.

Linux administration involves the management and maintenance of a Linux operating system. Here are some basic tasks involved in Linux administration:

1. **Installing and configuring the operating system**: The first step in Linux administration is installing the operating system on a computer or server. This involves selecting the appropriate distribution, creating installation media, and configuring the installation options.
2. **Managing user accounts and permissions**: Linux is a multi-user operating system, and as

such, it is necessary to create and manage user accounts and permissions. This includes creating new user accounts, assigning user groups, and managing user access permissions.

3. **Updating and patching the operating system:** Regular updates and patches are released to fix bugs and security vulnerabilities. It is important to keep the operating system up-to-date to ensure that it is secure and stable.

4. **Managing software packages**: Linux uses a package management system to install and manage software packages. Administrators need to be familiar with package management tools such as apt, yum, or pacman.

5. **Configuring system services**: Linux provides a wide range of services such as web servers, file servers, and email servers. Administrators need to know how to configure and manage these services.

6. **Monitoring system performance**: Monitoring the performance of a Linux system is important to ensure that it is running smoothly. This includes monitoring CPU usage, memory usage, disk usage, and network traffic.

7. **Troubleshooting system issues**: Linux administrators need to be able to diagnose and troubleshoot system issues when they arise. This involves using system logs, diagnostic tools, and other techniques to identify the root cause of the problem and resolve it.

These are just some of the basic tasks involved in Linux administration. As with any technical skill, there is always more to learn, and Linux administration is no exception.

Linux distributions, the Linux file system, and common administrative tasks:

1. Linux Distributions

Linux is an open-source operating system that comes in various distributions, or "distros," each with its own characteristics, features, and tools. Some of the popular Linux distributions include Ubuntu, Debian, Red Hat Enterprise Linux, Fedora, CentOS, and Arch Linux. Each distribution has its own package management system, user interface, and configuration tools.

Linux is an open-source operating system that comes in various distributions, also known as "distros," each with its own characteristics, features, and tools. The choice of a Linux distribution largely depends on the user's needs and preferences, such as ease of use, performance, stability, package management, software availability, and support.

Here are some of the popular Linux distributions:

1. **Ubuntu:** Ubuntu is a user-friendly and popular Linux distribution based on Debian. It has a simple and intuitive user interface and comes

with a variety of pre-installed software. It is suitable for both desktop and server use and is known for its regular releases and long-term support (LTS) versions.

2. **Debian**: Debian is a stable and reliable Linux distribution that is widely used in servers and workstations. It uses the APT (Advanced Package Tool) package management system and is known for its large and diverse software repository.

3. **Red Hat Enterprise Linux (RHEL):** RHEL is a popular and stable Linux distribution that is widely used in enterprise environments. It comes with advanced security features, support for virtualization and containers, and a comprehensive set of tools and services for system administration.

4. **Fedora**: Fedora is a community-driven Linux distribution that is known for its cutting-edge features and updates. It is suitable for both desktop and server use and comes with a variety of software packages and development tools.

5. **CentOS**: CentOS is a free and open-source Linux distribution based on RHEL. It is known for its stability and compatibility with RHEL packages and tools, and is widely used in servers and enterprise environments.

6. **Arch Linux**: Arch Linux is a lightweight and customizable Linux distribution that is suitable for advanced users and developers. It comes with a rolling-release model, which means that

the software is continuously updated and upgraded.

These are just a few examples of the many Linux distributions available, each with its own strengths and weaknesses. When choosing a Linux distribution, it is important to consider your needs, experience level, and support requirements.

2. **Linux File System**

The Linux file system is a hierarchical directory structure that organizes files and directories in a tree-like structure. The root directory, denoted by "/", is the top-level directory, which contains subdirectories such as /bin, /usr, /home, /var, and so on. Each directory can contain files, subdirectories, and symbolic links.

The Linux file system is a hierarchical directory structure that organizes and stores files and directories on a Linux-based operating system. The file system starts at the root directory (/), which is the highest level of the directory tree, and branches out to subdirectories and files.

Here are some of the key directories and their purposes in the Linux file system:

1. **/bin**: Contains essential executable files, such as system utilities and commands, that are required

for booting the system and running basic functions.

2. **/boot**: Contains files necessary for booting the system, such as the Linux kernel, bootloader, and initial RAM disk.

3. **/dev**: Contains device files that represent physical and virtual devices, such as hard drives, USB devices, and input/output devices.

4. **/etc:** Contains system configuration files that define system settings and parameters, such as network settings, user accounts, and system services.

5. **/home**: Contains user home directories, where user-specific files and settings are stored.

6. **/lib** and /lib64: Contains shared libraries that are necessary for running system programs and applications.

7. **/media**: Contains mount points for removable devices, such as CDs, DVDs, and USB drives.

8. **/opt**: Contains optional software packages and applications installed on the system.

9. **/proc**: Contains process information and system statistics, presented as files and directories.

10. **/root**: Contains the home directory for the root user.

11. **/sbin**: Contains essential system administration programs and commands that are not required for basic system functions.

12. **/tmp**: Contains temporary files created by the system and user programs.
13. **/usr:** Contains system-wide files and applications, such as user manuals, shared libraries, and executables.
14. **/var**: Contains variable data files, such as log files, spool files, and temporary files, that are constantly changing during system operation.

Understanding the Linux file system and its structure is important for system administration tasks such as managing disk space, configuring user accounts, and installing and updating software packages.

3. **Common Administrative Tasks**

Linux administrators are responsible for managing and maintaining Linux systems, which involves performing various administrative tasks, such as:

- **User and group management**: Creating and managing user accounts, setting permissions, and managing user groups.
- **Package management**: Installing, updating, and removing software packages using the package manager.
- **System monitoring**: Monitoring system performance, checking system logs, and identifying and resolving system issues.

- **System security:** Setting up firewalls, configuring security policies, and installing and configuring antivirus software.
- **Backups and recovery**: Creating and managing backups of system data and configuring recovery options.

Here are some common administrative tasks that are typically performed on a Linux system:

1. **User and Group Management**: Creating and managing user accounts and groups on the system, setting passwords, managing user access permissions, and modifying user properties.
2. **File and Directory Management**: Creating, deleting, renaming, copying, moving, and changing permissions of files and directories on the system.
3. **System Configuration:** Configuring system settings such as network interfaces, time zone, hostname, and startup services.
4. **Package Management**: Installing, updating, and removing software packages and dependencies using package managers such as apt, yum, or pacman.
5. **Backup and Restore**: Creating backups of system configurations, user data, and applications, and restoring them in case of system failure or data loss.
6. **Monitoring and Logging**: Monitoring system resources such as CPU, memory, and disk usage,

and analyzing system logs to identify errors and system issues.

7. **Security and Access Control**: Configuring firewall rules, managing user access permissions, and setting up secure connections such as SSH and SSL.

8. **System Updates and Maintenance:** Installing software updates and patches, maintaining system security, and performing system maintenance tasks such as disk defragmentation and file system checks.

In summary, Linux is a powerful and versatile operating system that comes in many distributions. The Linux file system is organized hierarchically and contains many directories and files. Linux administrators are responsible for performing various administrative tasks, including user and group management, package management, system monitoring, security management, and backups and recovery.

Real-world scenarios of common Linux administrative tasks:

1. **User and Group Management**: An organization needs to create new user accounts for new employees and grant them specific permissions and access levels to resources on the system. The Linux administrator creates the new user accounts, assigns them to the appropriate

groups, sets their passwords, and configures their access permissions.

2. **File and Directory Management**: A web server running on a Linux system needs to host multiple websites with different content and configurations. The Linux administrator creates separate directories for each website, sets appropriate permissions, and copies the website files and configurations to their respective directories.

3. **System Configuration**: A company has a fleet of Linux servers running different services, and the Linux administrator needs to ensure that all servers have the same configuration settings, such as hostname, network interface configurations, and startup services. The administrator uses configuration management tools such as Ansible or Puppet to automate the system configuration and ensure consistency across all servers.

4. **Package Management**: A Linux system needs to install and update software packages for different applications and services. The administrator uses the package manager, such as apt or yum, to install the required packages and dependencies and keep them up-to-date.

5. **Backup and Restore**: A company needs to ensure that all critical data and configurations on their Linux systems are backed up regularly to prevent data loss. The administrator configures automated backups using tools such as rsync or

tar and restores them in case of system failure or data loss.

6. **Monitoring and Logging**: A Linux system running critical services needs to be monitored for resource usage, system errors, and security threats. The administrator configures system monitoring tools such as Nagios or Zabbix to monitor the system and analyze system logs to identify and resolve issues.

7. **Security and Access Control**: A Linux system needs to be secured against unauthorized access and attacks. The administrator configures firewall rules, sets up secure connections using SSH and SSL, and manages user access permissions to prevent unauthorized access and ensure system security.

8. **System Updates and Maintenance**: A Linux system needs to be updated regularly with security patches, bug fixes, and software updates. The administrator schedules regular system maintenance tasks such as disk defragmentation and file system checks to ensure system stability and performance.

Questions and answers

1. What is Linux administration? Answer: Linux administration involves managing and maintaining Linux operating systems and associated software, including configuring system settings, installing and updating software

packages, managing users and groups, setting up and maintaining network services, and ensuring system security and stability.

2. What are some common Linux distributions? Answer: Some popular Linux distributions include Ubuntu, Debian, Red Hat Enterprise Linux (RHEL), Fedora, CentOS, and Arch Linux.

3. What is the Linux file system? Answer: The Linux file system is a hierarchical structure that organizes files and directories on a Linux system. It starts with the root directory ("/") and contains directories such as /bin, /etc, /home, /usr, and /var.

4. What are some common administrative tasks in Linux? Answer: Some common administrative tasks in Linux include user and group management, file and directory management, system configuration, package management, backup and restore, monitoring and logging, security and access control, and system updates and maintenance.

5. What are some tools for Linux administration? Answer: Some popular tools for Linux administration include the command-line interface (CLI), graphical user interface (GUI) tools such as GNOME and KDE, text editors such as Vim and Emacs, and system administration tools such as Ansible, Puppet, and Chef.

6. What skills are required for Linux administration? Answer: Linux administration requires skills in system administration, network

administration, scripting and automation, security, and troubleshooting, among others.

7. What are some resources for learning Linux administration? Answer: Some resources for learning Linux administration include online tutorials, documentation and manuals for various Linux distributions, forums and user groups, and training courses and certifications such as the Red Hat Certified System Administrator (RHCSA) and the Linux Professional Institute Certification (LPIC).

Common Administrative Tasks questions and answers

1. What is user management in Linux? Answer: User management in Linux involves creating, modifying, and deleting user accounts, assigning user privileges and permissions, and managing user groups.

2. What is package management in Linux? Answer: Package management in Linux involves installing, removing, and updating software packages, as well as resolving dependencies and managing package repositories.

3. What is file and directory management in Linux? Answer: File and directory management in Linux involves creating, modifying, and deleting files and directories, as well as managing file permissions and ownership.

4. What is system configuration in Linux? Answer: System configuration in Linux involves setting up and configuring system settings, such as network interfaces, hostname, time zone, and system services.

5. What is backup and restore in Linux? Answer: Backup and restore in Linux involves creating and restoring system backups, which can include files, directories, databases, and system configurations.

6. What is monitoring and logging in Linux? Answer: Monitoring and logging in Linux involves monitoring system performance, network activity, and system logs, as well as setting up alerts and notifications for critical events.

7. What is security and access control in Linux? Answer: Security and access control in Linux involves setting up and managing system security measures, such as firewalls, user authentication, and access controls, as well as configuring security policies and auditing system logs.

8. What is system updates and maintenance in Linux? Answer: System updates and maintenance in Linux involves installing security updates and patches, upgrading software packages, and performing routine system maintenance tasks.

9. What are some tools for Linux administrative tasks? Answer: Some popular tools for Linux

administrative tasks include the command-line interface (CLI), text editors such as Vim and Emacs, graphical user interface (GUI) tools such as GNOME and KDE, and system administration tools such as Ansible, Puppet, and Chef.

10. What skills are required for Linux administration? Answer: Linux administration requires skills in system administration, network administration, scripting and automation, security, and troubleshooting, among others. It also requires familiarity with Linux commands and utilities, package management, and system configuration.

Introduction to Linux glossary

1. **Linux**: A free and open-source operating system based on the Unix operating system.
2. **Distribution (distro):** A version of Linux that includes a specific collection of software packages and configuration settings.
3. **Kernel**: The core component of the Linux operating system that manages system resources and provides interfaces for applications.
4. **Shell**: A command-line interface that allows users to interact with the operating system and execute commands.
5. **Bash**: A popular shell program for Linux that is known for its powerful scripting capabilities.

6. **Filesystem**: A structure that organizes and stores files and directories on a storage device.
7. **Package**: A software package that contains one or more programs, libraries, or other resources.
8. **Repository**: A collection of packages that are available for installation and updating through a package manager.
9. **Package manager**: A tool that allows users to install, remove, and update software packages, as well as manage package repositories.
10. **Root**: The administrative user account in Linux with full system privileges.
11. **User**: A non-administrative account in Linux that can perform certain tasks and access specific files and directories.
12. **Shell script**: A program written in a shell language that automates tasks or performs system administration tasks.
13. **Command**: An instruction given to the operating system to perform a specific action.
14. **Daemon**: A background process that runs continuously and provides specific services or functions.
15. **Service**: A program or set of programs that provide specific functionality or support to other programs or users.
16. **Firewall**: A security measure that blocks unauthorized access to a system by filtering network traffic.

17. SSH: A secure network protocol that allows users to securely connect to a remote system and execute commands.
18. **File permissions**: A set of access rights that determine which users or groups can read, write, or execute files and directories.
19. **Cron**: A system utility that allows users to schedule and automate recurring tasks.
20. **RAID**: A data storage technology that combines multiple physical disks into a single logical unit for improved performance, reliability, or both.

An Introduction to Linux Basics

Linux is a family of free and open-source operating systems based on the Linux kernel. Operating systems based on Linux are known as *Linux distributions* or *distros*. Examples include Debian, Ubuntu, Fedora, CentOS, Gentoo, Arch Linux, and many others.

The Linux kernel has been under active development since 1991, and has proven to be extremely versatile and adaptable. You can find computers that run Linux in a wide variety of contexts all over the world, from web servers to cell phones. Today, 90% of all cloud infrastructure and 74% of the world's smartphones are powered by Linux.

However, newcomers to Linux may find it somewhat difficult to approach, as Linux filesystems have a different structure than those found on Windows or MacOS. Additionally, Linux-based operating systems depend heavily on working with the command line interface, while most personal computers rely on graphical interfaces.

This guide serves as an introduction to important command line concepts and skills and equips newcomers to learn more about Linux.

Prerequisites

To follow along with this guide, you will need access to a computer running a Linux-based operating system. This can either be a virtual private server which you've connected to with SSH or your local machine. Note that this tutorial was validated using a Linux server running Ubuntu 20.04, but the examples given should work on a computer running any version of any Linux distribution.

The Terminal

The terms "terminal," "shell," and "command line interface" are often used interchangeably, but there are subtle differences between them:

- A *terminal* is an input and output environment that presents a text-only window running a shell.
- A *shell* is a program that exposes the computer's operating system to a user or program. In Linux

systems, the shell presented in a terminal is a command line interpreter.

- **A *command line interface*** is a user interface (managed by a command line interpreter program) which processes commands to a computer program and outputs the results.

When someone refers to one of these three terms in the context of Linux, they generally mean a terminal environment where you can run commands and see the results printed out to the terminal, such as this:

Becoming a Linux expert requires you to be comfortable with using a terminal. Any administrative task, including file manipulation, package installation, and user management, can be accomplished through the terminal. The terminal is interactive: you specify commands to run and the terminal outputs the results of those commands. To execute any command, you type it into the prompt and press ENTER.

When accessing a cloud server, you'll most often be doing so through a terminal shell. Although personal computers that run Linux often come with the kind of graphical desktop environment familiar to most computer users, it is often more efficient or practical to perform certain tasks through commands entered into the terminal.

The Filesystem Hierarchy Standard

Nearly all Linux distributions are compliant with a universal standard for filesystem directory structure known as the Filesystem Hierarchy Standard (FHS). The FHS defines a set of directories, each of which serve their own special function.

The forward slash (/) is used to indicate the root directory in the filesystem hierarchy defined by the FHS.

When a user logs in to the shell, they are brought to their own user directory, stored within /home/. This is referred to as the user's *home directory*. The FHS defines /home/ as containing the home directories for regular users.

The **root** user has its own home directory specified by the FHS: /root/. Note that / is referred to as the "root directory", and that it is different from root/, which is stored within /.

Because the FHS is the default filesystem layout on Linux machines, and each directory within it is included to serve a specific purpose, it simplifies the process of organizing files by their function.

Navigation

Linux filesystems are based on a directory tree. This means that you can create directories (which are functionally identical to *folders* found in other operating systems) inside other directories, and files can exist in any directory.

To see what directory you are currently active in you can run the pwd command, which stands for "print working directory":

```
1.  pwd
2.
```

pwd prints the path to your current directory. The output will be similar to this:

```
Output

/home/sammy
```

This example output indicates that the current active directory is sammy, which is inside the home/ directory, which lives in the root directory, /. As mentioned previously, since the sammy/ directory is stored within the home/ directory, sammy/ represents the **sammy** user's home directory.

To see a list of files and directories that exist in your current working directory, run the ls command:

```
1.  ls
2.
```

This will return a list of the names of any files or directories held in your current working directory. If you're following this guide on a new machine, though, this command may not return any output.

You can create one or more new directories within your current working directory with the mkdir command, which stands for "make directory". For example, to create two new directories named testdir1 and testdir2, you might run the following command:

```
1.  mkdir testdir1 testdir2
2.
```

Now when you run the ls command, these directories will appear in the output:

```
1.  ls
2.
```

```
Output

testdir1

testdir2
```

To navigate into one of these new directories, run the cd command (which stands for "change directory") and specify the directory's name:

```
1.  cd testdir1
2.
```

This will change your new current working directory to the directory you specified. You can see this with pwd:

```
1.  pwd
2.
```

```
Output

/home/sammy/testdir1
```

However, because testdir1 and testdir2 are both held in the **sammy** user's home directory, they reside in different branches of the directory tree.
The cd command looks for directories within your current working directory, so this means that you cannot cd directly into the testdir2 directory you created previously while testdir1 is your working directory:

```
1.  cd testdir2
2.
```

Output

bash: cd: testdir2: No such file or directory

However, you can navigate into any existing directory regardless of your current working directory if you specify the full path of the directory you want to navigate to:

```
1.  cd /home/sammy/testdir2
2.
```

Copy

Note: In Linux, a tilde (~) is shorthand for the home directory of the user you're logged in as. Knowing this, you could alternatively write the previous command like this and it would achieve the same result:

```
1.  cd ~/testdir2
2.
```

Additionally, you can specify .. to change to the directory one level up in your path. To get back to your original directory:

```
1.  cd ..
2.
```

If you're ever confused about where you are in the navigation tree, remember you can always run the pwd command to find your current directory. Many modern shells (including Bash, the default for many Linux distributions) also indicate your current directory, as exhibited in the example commands throughout this section.

File Manipulation

You cannot use cd to interact with files; cd stands for "change directory", and only allows you to navigate directories. You can, however, create, edit, and view the contents of files.

One way to create a file is with the touch command. To create a new file called file.txt:

```
1.  touch file.txt
2.
```

This creates an empty file with the name file.txt in your current working directory. The contents of this file are empty.

If you decide to rename file.txt later on, you can do so with the mv command:

```
1.  mv file.txt newfile.txt
2.
```

mv stands for "move" and it can move a file or directory from one place to another. By specifying the original file, file.txt, you can "move" it to a new location in the current working directory, thereby renaming it.

It is also possible to copy a file to a new location with the cp command. If we want to bring back file.txt but keep newfile.txt, you can make a copy of newfile.txt named file.txt like this:

```
1.  cp newfile.txt file.txt
2.
```

As you may have guessed, cp is short for "copy". By copying newfile.txt to a new file called file.txt, you have replicated the original file in a new file with a different name.

However, files are not of much use if they don't contain anything. To edit files, a file editor is necessary.

There are many options for file editors, all created by professionals for daily use. Such editors include vim, emacs, nano, and pico.

nano is a suitable option for beginners: it is relatively user-friendly and doesn't overload you with cryptic options or commands.

To add text to file.txt with nano, run the following command:

```
1.  nano file.txt
2.
```

This will open up a space where you can immediately start typing to edit file.txt. Add whatever text you like, or you can copy the text in this example:

file.txt

Say it's only a paper moon
Sailing over a cardboard sea,
But it wouldn't be make believe
If you believed in me.

Yes it's only a canvas sky
Hanging over a muslin tree,
But it wouldn't be make believe
If you believed in me.

Without your love,
It's a honky-tonk parade.
Without your love,
It's a melody played in a penny arcade.

It's a Barnum and Bailey world,
Just as phony as it can be,
But it wouldn't be make believe
If you believed in me.

To save your written text, press CTRL + X, Y, and then ENTER. This returns you to the shell with a newly saved file.txt file.

Now that file.txt has some text within it, you can view it using cat or less.

The cat command prints the contents of a specified file to your system's output. Try running cat and pass the file.txt file you just edited as an argument:

```
1.  cat file.txt
2.
```

This will print out the entire contents of file.txt to the terminal. If you used the text from the previous example, this command will return output similar to this:

```
Output

Say it's only a paper moon

Sailing over a cardboard sea,

But it wouldn't be make believe

If you believed in me.


Yes it's only a canvas sky
```

Hanging over a muslin tree,

But it wouldn't be make believe

If you believed in me.

Without your love,

It's a honky-tonk parade.

Without your love,

It's a melody played in a penny arcade.

It's a Barnum and Bailey world,

Just as phony as it can be,

But it wouldn't be make believe

If you believed in me.

Using cat to view file contents can be unwieldy and difficult to read if the file is particularly long. As an alternative, you can use the less command which will allow you to paginate the output.

Use less to view the contents of the file.txt file, like this:

```
1.  less file.txt
```

```
2.
```

This will also print the contents of file.txt, but one terminal page at a time beginning at the start of the file. You can use the spacebar to advance a page, or the arrow keys to go up and down one line at a time.

Press q to quit out of less.

Finally, to delete the file.txt file, pass the name of the file as an argument to rm:

```
1.  rm file.txt
2.
```

Copy

Note: Without other options, the rm command (which stands for "remove") cannot be used to delete directories. However, it does include the -d flag which allows you to delete empty directories:

```
1.  rm -d directory
2.
```

Copy

You can also remove empty directories with the rmdir command:

```
1.  rmdir directory
2.
```

Copy

If you want to delete a directory that isn't empty, you can run rm with the -r flag. This will delete the specified directory along with of its contents, including any files and subdirectories:

```
1.  rm -r directory
2.
```

Copy

However, because deleting content is a permanent action, you should **only run rm with the -r option if you're certain that you want to delete the specified directory**.

To see the man page for any command, pass the command's name as an argument to the man command:

```
1.  man command
2.
```

For instance, man rm displays the purpose of rm, how to use it, what options are available, examples of use, and more useful information.

CHAPTER 2: ESSENTIAL LINUX ADMINISTRATION SKILLS

Linux administration is the process of managing and maintaining Linux systems, which are based on the Linux operating system. Linux is an open-source operating system that is used in a wide range of applications, from personal computers to large-scale servers and data centers.

Linux administrators are responsible for tasks such as system installation, configuration, maintenance, and troubleshooting. They ensure that the system is running efficiently and effectively, and that it is secure from unauthorized access and other security threats.

Linux is one of the most popular and widely used operating systems in the world, powering servers, desktops, mobile devices, and embedded systems. Essential Linux administration skills are important for anyone who wants to work with Linux systems, whether it's for personal use or in a professional setting.

Here are some of the essential Linux administration skills:

1. Installation and configuration: Installing Linux on a computer or server requires knowledge of hardware compatibility, partitioning, and filesystems. Configuration involves setting up

users, permissions, network interfaces, and other system settings.

2. Command-line basics: The Linux command line is a powerful tool for managing and manipulating files, processes, and system settings. Learning basic command-line skills is essential for any Linux administrator.

3. **Package management**: Linux systems use package managers to install, update, and remove software packages. Understanding how to use package managers is essential for maintaining a stable and secure system.

4. **System monitoring and troubleshooting**: Linux administrators need to be able to monitor system performance, troubleshoot issues, and resolve errors. This involves using system logs, monitoring tools, and command-line utilities.

5. **Security and permissions**: Linux systems have a robust security model that includes user accounts, permissions, firewalls, and other security features. Understanding how to configure and manage security settings is essential for maintaining the integrity of the system.

6. **Network configuration:** Linux systems are often used as servers and require network configuration to provide services such as web hosting, file sharing, and remote access. Understanding how to configure network interfaces, firewalls, and services is essential for network administrators.

linux administration real world scenario

One real-world scenario of Linux administration could be in a web hosting company that provides shared hosting services to clients. In this scenario, the Linux administrator would be responsible for managing the Linux servers that host client websites and ensuring that they run smoothly and securely.

Some of the tasks that a Linux administrator would perform in this scenario include:

1. Installing and configuring Linux on the servers.
2. Installing and configuring web server software, such as Apache or Nginx, to serve client websites.
3. Configuring database software, such as MySQL or PostgreSQL, to support client applications.
4. Creating and managing user accounts and permissions for clients to access their hosting accounts.
5. Monitoring system performance and resource usage to ensure that clients' websites are responsive and fast.
6. Maintaining system security through the use of firewalls, intrusion detection systems, and other security measures to prevent unauthorized access to client data.
7. Managing system backups and recovery operations to ensure that client data is protected in the event of system failures or disasters.

8. Troubleshooting system issues and resolving problems as they arise to ensure that clients' websites are always available and functioning correctly.

1. Installing and configuring Linux on the servers.

Installing and configuring Linux on servers is a critical task in Linux administration, as it forms the foundation for all other tasks that a Linux administrator will perform. Here are the general steps for installing and configuring Linux on servers:

1. **Choose the Linux distribution**: There are many different Linux distributions available, each with its own set of features and capabilities. Choose the distribution that best meets the needs of your organization.
2. **Prepare the installation media**: Download the installation media for your chosen Linux distribution, and create a bootable USB drive or DVD.
3. **Boot the server from the installation media**: Insert the bootable media into the server, and restart the server. Follow the prompts to boot from the media.
4. Begin the installation process: Once the server has booted from the installation media, follow the prompts to begin the installation process. This may involve partitioning the hard drive,

selecting packages to install, and configuring basic system settings.

5. **Configure network settings**: Once the installation is complete, configure the network settings for the server, including IP address, hostname, and DNS settings.

6. **Install and configure necessary software packages**: Depending on the intended use of the server, install and configure the necessary software packages, such as web servers, database servers, and other services.

7. **Configure security settings**: Linux servers have a robust security model that includes user accounts, permissions, and firewalls. Configure the security settings for the server to ensure that it is secure from unauthorized access and other security threats.

8. **Test the server**: Once the installation and configuration are complete, test the server to ensure that it is functioning correctly and that all services are accessible.

Installing and configuring a web server software, such as Apache or Nginx, is a key task in Linux administration when hosting client websites. Here are the general steps for installing and configuring a web server:

1. **Install the web server software**: Use the package manager of your Linux distribution to

install the web server software. For example, to install Apache on Ubuntu, you can run the command **sudo apt-get install apache2**.

2. **Configure the web server**: Once the web server software is installed, configure it to serve client websites. This may involve configuring virtual hosts, which allow multiple websites to be hosted on the same server. For example, you can create a virtual host for a website by creating a new configuration file in the **/etc/apache2/sites-available/** directory.

3. **Test the web server**: Once the web server is configured, test it to ensure that it is serving websites correctly. You can test this by accessing the website using a web browser, or by using command-line tools such as **curl** or **wget**.

4. **Configure security settings:** Web servers can be vulnerable to various security threats, such as attacks on the web server software itself or attacks on websites hosted on the server. Configure the security settings for the web server to ensure that it is secure from these threats. This may involve configuring firewalls, setting up SSL certificates, and implementing other security measures.

5. **Monitor the web server**: Monitor the web server to ensure that it is performing well and to detect any issues that may arise. This can be done using various monitoring tools, such as Nagios, Zabbix, or Prometheus.

3. Configuring database software, such as MySQL or PostgreSQL, to support client applications.

Configuring a database software like MySQL or PostgreSQL to support client applications involves a few steps. Here's a general overview of the process:

1. **Install the database software**: Begin by installing the database software on the server where the database will be hosted. Follow the installation instructions for your particular database software.
2. **Create a database**: After installing the database software, create a new database. This will be the location where your data will be stored.
3. **Create a user account**: Create a user account with appropriate permissions to access the database. Depending on the level of access required by the client application, you may need to create multiple user accounts.
4. **Configure the database server**: Configure the database server to listen to incoming client connections. This typically involves opening up the appropriate network ports and configuring the firewall settings.
5. **Configure the client application**: Finally, configure the client application to connect to the database. This typically involves specifying the database server's IP address, port number, and user credentials.

4. Creating and managing user accounts and permissions for clients to access their hosting accounts with steps

Creating and managing user accounts and permissions for clients to access their hosting accounts involves a few steps. Here's a general overview of the process:

1. **Create a hosting account**: Begin by creating a hosting account for the client. This typically involves selecting a hosting plan, registering a domain name, and configuring the hosting environment.
2. **Create a user account**: Once the hosting account has been created, create a user account for the client. This will allow the client to log in and manage their hosting account.
3. **Set permissions**: Configure the user account permissions based on the client's needs. This may include granting access to certain files or directories, allowing access to specific software or tools, or enabling certain server settings.
4. **Provide login credentials**: Provide the client with their login credentials, including their username and password. It's important to ensure that these credentials are secure and not easily guessable.
5. **Train the client**: If necessary, provide training to the client on how to use the hosting account and any associated tools or software.

6. **Monitor usage**: Monitor the client's usage of the hosting account and adjust permissions as needed. This may involve revoking permissions if the client no longer needs them or granting additional permissions if the client's needs change.

7. **Ensure security**: Ensure that appropriate security measures are in place to protect the client's data and prevent unauthorized access. This may include enabling SSL/TLS encryption, configuring firewalls, and implementing strong password policies.

5. Monitoring system performance and resource usage to ensure that clients' websites are responsive and fast.

Monitoring system performance and resource usage is crucial to ensure that clients' websites are responsive and fast. Here are some steps you can take to monitor system performance and resource usage:

1. Set up monitoring tools: Install and configure monitoring tools to track system performance metrics such as CPU usage, memory usage, disk I/O, network traffic, and server uptime.

2. **Define performance thresholds**: Define performance thresholds for each metric to alert you when resource usage exceeds acceptable levels. This will help you identify potential issues before they impact website performance.

3. **Analyze performance data**: Analyze performance data regularly to identify trends and patterns that may indicate underlying issues. Look for anomalies in resource usage that could be causing slow website performance.

4. **Optimize server settings**: Optimize server settings such as caching, compression, and database configuration to improve website performance. Ensure that your server is running the latest version of the software and that all updates and patches have been applied.

5. **Monitor website response time**: Monitor website response time using tools such as website monitoring services or web analytics tools. This will help you identify any issues that may be impacting website performance.

6. **Investigate performance issues**: Investigate performance issues promptly when they are detected. Use the monitoring data to identify the root cause of the issue and take appropriate action to resolve it.

6. Maintaining system security through the use of firewalls, intrusion detection systems, and other security measures to prevent unauthorized access to client data.

Maintaining system security is crucial to prevent unauthorized access to client data. Here are some steps you can take to maintain system security:

1. **Install a firewall**: Install a firewall to monitor incoming and outgoing network traffic and block unauthorized access attempts. Configure the firewall to allow only necessary ports and services.

2. **Implement intrusion detection systems:** Implement intrusion detection systems to detect and respond to unauthorized access attempts. Configure the intrusion detection system to alert you when suspicious activity is detected.

3. **Use secure authentication methods**: Use secure authentication methods such as two-factor authentication to prevent unauthorized access to client accounts. Encourage clients to use strong passwords and change them regularly.

4. **Use encryption**: Use encryption to protect sensitive data such as client passwords and credit card information. Ensure that SSL/TLS is enabled on your web server to encrypt data in transit.

5. **Keep software up to date**: Keep software up to date with the latest security patches and updates. Apply security patches promptly to prevent exploitation of known vulnerabilities.

6. **Use security best practices**: Follow security best practices such as least privilege access and principle of least privilege. Ensure that only authorized personnel have access to sensitive data.

7. **Perform regular security audits**: Perform regular security audits to identify vulnerabilities and areas for improvement. Conduct penetration testing to identify potential weaknesses in your security measures.

7. Managing system backups and recovery operations to ensure that client data is protected in the event of system failures or disasters.

Managing system backups and recovery operations is an important aspect of ensuring that client data is protected in the event of system failures or disasters. Here are some key steps to consider when managing system backups and recovery:

1. **Develop a backup plan**: Start by developing a comprehensive backup plan that identifies the critical data that needs to be backed up, the frequency of backups, the backup storage location, and the retention period for backups.
2. **Automate backups**: Use automated backup tools to schedule regular backups and ensure that backups are performed consistently and reliably.
3. Test backups: Regularly test your backups to ensure that they can be successfully restored in the event of a system failure or disaster.
4. **Store backups securely**: Store backups in a secure location that is physically separate from the primary data storage location. This will help

ensure that backups are not affected by the same disasters or failures that may impact the primary data storage.

5. **Develop a recovery plan**: Develop a recovery plan that outlines the steps that need to be taken to recover data in the event of a system failure or disaster.

6. **Test the recovery plan**: Regularly test the recovery plan to ensure that it can be executed effectively in the event of a real disaster or system failure.

7. **Update the backup and recovery plan**: Regularly review and update your backup and recovery plan to ensure that it remains relevant and effective as your system and data storage needs evolve.

By following these steps, you can effectively manage system backups and recovery operations to protect client data and ensure business continuity in the event of system failures or disasters.

Essential Linux Administration key words

Here are some essential Linux administration keywords:

1. **Kernel**: The core component of the Linux operating system that manages system resources, such as memory and CPU time.

2. **Shell**: The command-line interface that allows users to interact with the Linux operating system.
3. **Filesystem**: The hierarchical organization of files and directories on a Linux system.
4. **User accounts**: The individual accounts created for each user on a Linux system, which determine their access permissions and settings.
5. **Permissions**: The settings that determine who can read, write, or execute a particular file or directory on a Linux system.
6. **Packages**: The software packages that can be installed on a Linux system to add new functionality or features.
7. **Services**: The background processes that run on a Linux system to provide specific functions, such as web servers or database servers.
8. **Networking**: The configuration and management of network connections on a Linux system.
9. Security: The measures taken to secure a Linux system from unauthorized access or attacks.
10. **System logs**: The records of system events and activities that can be used for troubleshooting and monitoring purposes.

Chapter 3 : Best Practices for Linux Administration

The best practices for Linux administration have evolved over time as the Linux operating system and associated tools have developed and matured. Here's a brief history:

1. In the early days of Linux, administration was largely done through the command line, and best practices focused on using the available command line tools to configure and manage the system.
2. As graphical user interfaces (GUIs) became more common, best practices evolved to include using GUI-based tools to simplify administration tasks.
3. With the rise of virtualization and containerization technologies, best practices evolved to focus on using these technologies to improve system scalability and isolation.
4. As Linux became more widely used in enterprise environments, best practices evolved to include compliance with industry regulations and standards, such as HIPAA and PCI DSS.
5. More recently, best practices have shifted towards using automation tools, such as Ansible and Puppet, to simplify and streamline administration tasks and improve consistency and repeatability.

why Best Practices for Linux Administration?

Using best practices for Linux administration is important for several reasons:

1. **Security**: Linux systems are a common target for hackers and cybercriminals, and following best practices can help reduce the risk of unauthorized access, data breaches, and other security threats.
2. **Stability**: Linux systems can be complex, and proper administration can help ensure that the system remains stable and reliable over time.
3. **Performance**: Properly configuring and optimizing a Linux system can help improve performance and scalability, allowing the system to handle more workload.
4. **Compliance**: Many industries and organizations are subject to regulations that require secure and compliant system administration practices. Following best practices can help ensure compliance with these regulations.
5. **Disaster recovery**: Proper backup and disaster recovery planning can help minimize the impact of system failures or disasters and ensure that critical data is protected and recoverable.

Chapter 4 : Advanced Linux Administration

Advanced Linux administration refers to the management and configuration of complex Linux systems and networks that require a high level of technical skill and expertise. This includes managing and optimizing the Linux kernel, configuring and securing network services, managing storage systems, implementing high availability and clustering technologies, monitoring system performance, and automating routine tasks.

Advanced Linux administrators typically have a deep understanding of Linux systems and technologies, as well as experience in managing and troubleshooting complex systems and networks. They are often responsible for designing and implementing complex solutions that support business critical applications and services, and ensuring that these systems are highly available, secure, and performant.

Overall, advanced Linux administration requires a broad range of technical skills and experience, and is a key area of expertise for many IT professionals and organizations that rely on Linux systems to support their operations.

Advanced Linux administration involves the management and configuration of complex Linux systems and networks, and requires a deep understanding of the underlying technologies and architectures. Here are some key skills and topics that are typically covered in advanced Linux administration:

1. **Kernel tuning and optimization:** Advanced Linux administrators need to understand how to optimize the Linux kernel to improve system performance and scalability, including configuring kernel parameters and modules.

2. **Network configuration and management**: Advanced Linux administrators need to be familiar with network protocols, services, and technologies, and be able to configure and manage network interfaces, routing, firewalls, and other network components.

3. **Storage management:** Advanced Linux administrators need to understand how to manage storage systems, including RAID, LVM, and file systems, and be able to configure and manage storage devices, partitions, and volumes.

4. **High availability and clustering**: Advanced Linux administrators need to be able to configure and manage high availability and clustering technologies, such as Pacemaker and Corosync, to ensure system reliability and uptime.

5. **Security and compliance**: Advanced Linux administrators need to be familiar with security best practices and compliance regulations, and be able to implement and manage security controls such as firewalls, intrusion detection and prevention systems, and encryption.

6. **Performance monitoring and tuning**: Advanced Linux administrators need to be able to monitor system performance and identify

performance bottlenecks, and be able to use performance tuning tools and techniques to optimize system performance.

7. **Scripting and automation**: Advanced Linux administrators need to be familiar with scripting and automation tools such as Bash, Python, and Ansible, and be able to write scripts and automate tasks to improve efficiency and consistency.

advanced topics in Linux administration, such as kernel tuning, configuring security settings, and managing services and daemons.

In addition to kernel tuning, configuring security settings, and managing services and daemons, here are some other advanced topics in Linux administration:

1. **Containerization**: Advanced Linux administrators need to be familiar with containerization technologies such as Docker and Kubernetes, and be able to configure and manage containerized applications and services.

2. **Virtualization**: Advanced Linux administrators need to be able to configure and manage virtualization technologies such as KVM, Xen, and VMware, and be able to optimize virtualized environments for performance and scalability.

3. **Cloud computing**: Advanced Linux administrators need to be familiar with cloud computing technologies such as Amazon Web

Services (AWS), Microsoft Azure, and Google Cloud Platform (GCP), and be able to configure and manage Linux instances in cloud environments.

4. **Monitoring and logging**: Advanced Linux administrators need to be able to monitor system performance and identify issues using tools such as Nagios, Zabbix, and Prometheus, and be able to collect and analyse system logs using tools such as Logstash, Fluentd, and Elasticsearch.

5. Configuration management: Advanced Linux administrators need to be able to use configuration management tools such as Ansible, Puppet, and Chef, to automate the configuration and management of Linux systems and services.

6. Scripting and programming: Advanced Linux administrators need to be proficient in scripting and programming languages such as Bash, Python, Perl, and Ruby, and be able to write scripts and programs to automate tasks, extend system functionality, and build custom tools.

Chapter 5: Troubleshooting Linux Systems

why Troubleshooting Linux Systems ?

Troubleshooting Linux systems is important because it allows Linux administrators to identify and resolve issues that may affect system performance, reliability, and security. Linux systems are widely used in many different industries and applications, from web servers and cloud computing to scientific research and embedded devices, and are often critical to the success of these applications and services.

As with any complex technology, Linux systems are prone to issues and errors that may impact system performance and availability. These issues can arise from a variety of factors, including hardware failures, software bugs, configuration errors, security vulnerabilities, and external threats.

Effective troubleshooting helps Linux administrators quickly identify and resolve issues, minimize system downtime and data loss, and ensure that critical systems and services remain available and reliable. Troubleshooting also helps administrators proactively identify and address potential issues before they become major problems, and helps organizations maintain the high levels of system performance and availability that are essential for their success.

Troubleshooting Linux systems is a critical skill for Linux administrators and involves identifying and resolving issues that may arise with system hardware, software, or configuration. Here are some key steps in troubleshooting Linux systems:

1. **Identify the problem:** The first step in troubleshooting is to identify the problem by gathering information about symptoms, error messages, and system behavior. This may involve reviewing system logs, checking system performance metrics, and performing system tests or diagnostics.

2. **Define the problem**: Once the problem has been identified, the next step is to define the problem in more detail, including its root cause and impact on system functionality.

3. **Develop a plan**: Based on the problem definition, the Linux administrator needs to develop a plan for resolving the issue. This may involve implementing a temporary workaround, applying a patch or update, or reconfiguring system settings.

4. **Test the solution**: After implementing a solution, it is important to test the system to ensure that the problem has been resolved and that system functionality has been restored.

5. **Document the solution**: Once the problem has been resolved, it is important to document the solution, including any changes made to system settings or configurations, to help prevent similar issues from occurring in the future.

Some common issues that may need troubleshooting in Linux systems include:

1.	Kernel panics or crashes
2.	Networking issues, such as DNS or routing problems
3.	Disk and file system errors
4.	Security vulnerabilities and breaches
5.	Application errors or crashes
6.	Performance and scalability issues

To be effective at troubleshooting Linux systems, administrators need a deep understanding of Linux architecture, as well as experience in managing and troubleshooting complex systems and networks. They also need to be familiar with a wide range of tools and techniques for diagnosing and resolving system issues, including system logs, debugging tools, and diagnostic utilities.

Troubleshooting Linux Systems key words

Here are some key words related to troubleshooting Linux systems:

- **Diagnostics**: The process of identifying and analyzing problems or issues with a system or component.

- Logs: A record of system events, such as error messages, that can be used to help diagnose and troubleshoot issues.
- **Debugging**: The process of identifying and resolving errors or defects in software or hardware components.
- Root cause analysis: The process of identifying the underlying cause of a problem or issue, rather than just addressing its symptoms.
- **Performance metrics**: Measurements of system performance, such as CPU usage, memory usage, and network bandwidth, that can be used to identify and troubleshoot performance issues.
- **Patching and updates**: The process of applying software updates or patches to fix known issues or vulnerabilities in a system or component.
- **Security vulnerabilities**: Weaknesses in a system or component that can be exploited by attackers to gain unauthorized access or cause damage to the system.
- **Configuration management**: The process of managing system settings and configurations to ensure that they are accurate and up-to-date, and to prevent issues caused by misconfigurations.
- Disaster recovery: The process of restoring system functionality and data in the event of a catastrophic failure or disaster, such as a system crash or natural disaster.

Mastering Linux Administration: Essential Skills and Best Practices glossary

Here is a glossary of terms related to mastering Linux administration:

- **Bash**: A popular shell or command-line interface for Linux and Unix systems.
- **Daemon**: A background process that runs continuously on a system and provides a particular service or functionality.
- **Filesystem**: A hierarchical organization of files and directories used to store and manage data on a Linux system.
- **Kernel**: The core component of the Linux operating system that interacts directly with hardware and provides essential system services.
- **Package manager**: A software tool used to install, update, and manage packages or software applications on a Linux system.
- **Root**: The highest level of access or privilege on a Linux system, often reserved for system administrators.
- **Shell**: A command-line interface that provides a way to interact with a Linux system and execute commands and scripts.
- **Systemd**: A system and service manager used in many modern Linux distributions to manage system startup, services, and processes.

- **Terminal**: A text-based interface used to interact with a Linux system, often accessed through a shell or terminal emulator.
- **User account**: A named account associated with a specific user on a Linux system, used to manage access and permissions for that user.
- **Virtualization**: The process of creating virtualized versions of hardware, operating systems, or applications to enable better resource utilization and flexibility in a computing environment.
- **YUM**: The Yellowdog Updater, Modified (YUM) is a package manager used in some Linux distributions to manage software packages and dependencies.
- **ZFS**: The Z File System (ZFS) is a file system and volume manager used in some Linux distributions that provides advanced features such as data integrity, data compression, and snapshotting.

Linux Tools for Network Troubleshooting

We want to look at some basic network commands that you must understand in order to write the Linux+ exam. They are ping, ifconfig, and tracert. These are fundamental troubleshooting tools that will help you find issues on a network.

ping

Any basic network troubleshooting starts with the ping command, no matter which operating system or platform you use. To use it in Linux, simply drop into a terminal and run the command with a target IP address. Below is an example of how to use the command if our target IP address is 192.168.1.1.

ping 192.168.1.1

Ping in Linux runs indefinitely, so you have to CTRL+C to stop the command. If you would like ping to act more like it does in the Windows operating system then you can run it like this:

ping -c 4 192.168.1.1

Running it with a -c switch enables the routing compartment identifier, while the 4 tells ping to run four times before stopping.

If you find that your network is unreachable, and that your computer/server is also unreachable to the rest of the network, then you might be dealing with a local network issue.

ifconfig

If you are certain that your network cable is connected, and that you have a physical connection to your network switch or router, then you can proceed to checking out the system configuration of your local device. Luckily there is an easy way to do this from the command line in Linux. All we need to do is drop into the terminal and type in the following:

ifconfig

You will get an output that highlights all of your active network connections. If you are using a wired connection then you should see an eth0 or eth1 depending on your setup and how many network cards you have. If you are using a wireless card, then you can look for wlan0 as your wireless adapter. In our example we are looking at eth0, and our IP address is 192.168.1.111. We have removed the mac address from this output, but you can find yours by using this command.

eth0: flags=4163<UP,BROADCAST,RUNNING,MULTIC AST> mtu 1500
    inet 192.168.1.111 netmask 255.255.255.0 broadcast 192.168.1.255
    inet6 fe80::3eb7:dd41:2b6d:1e28 prefixlen 64 scopeid 0x20<link>
    ether ############ txqueuelen 1000 (Ethernet)
    RX packets 6163515 bytes 6369685703 (5.9 GiB)
    RX errors 0 dropped 0 overruns 0 frame 0
    TX packets 2803165 bytes 438330018 (418.0 MiB)
    TX errors 0 dropped 0 overruns 0 carrier 0 collisions 0
traceroute

If you have a connection to your router, but you can't seem to connect to the internet, or to another target computer on another segment of your network, then you can use the traceroute command. A common technique when troubleshooting internet issues is to try and contact a Google DNS server. This is because Google has incredible uptime, so the chances of this target being offline is very, very slim. From the terminal, type the following:

traceroute 8.8.8.8

You will get an output that shows all of the different hops that your data is taking to get onto the internet. If your connection is being blocked, or if it is failing on its way to the target, then you will see which device is causing the issue.

Linux Boot Issue Troubleshooting: An Example

Not all Linux boot issues are catastrophic, which is a good thing! Sometimes you may want to find out what an error message is pointing to, or why a service is failing on boot. Anything that makes the system run less than optimal.

In most cases you will be able to find some great information about your system by looking at the boot.log file on your computer or server. Some of these files require root access, so you may need to run the sudo command in front of these examples. And know what your root password is. If you do not have access to a graphical desktop then you can easily read the contents of your file by simply typing the following **from a command line:**

cat /var/log/boot.log

This will output the contents of the log file by using the concatenate command (cat). If you wanted to see only the newest or the oldest contents of the file quickly then you could type either of the following:

head /var/log/boot.log

Head for the first 10 lines of the file

tail /var/log/boot.log

Tail for the last 10 lines of the file

The same goes for the /var/log/messages file as well, as it can contain helpful messages about why your system is experiencing boot issues. If your system is running a later version of Linux and you are able to get to a command line, then you can run the command journalctl.

journalctl

Running this command will give you an output from the SystemD logs, and it can help you to pinpoint the exact issue that is plaguing your system.

One of the advantages of Linux for administrators is the fact that it stores so much information about the current state of the machine that it is running on. This is very valuable when you run into boot issues that are preventing the system from booting up.

Even better is the fact that most of the log files are stored as plain text, so even if you are unable to boot the system up into a shell environment then you will still be able to do some investigative digging on the system.

Linux File System Troubleshooting: An Example

Sometimes you might experience a hard disk failure while using your Linux machine. This is terrifying enough on most systems, but in Linux the perception is that it can be especially tough to deal with. However this is not the case, as there are a lot of different tools that we can use to chase down the culprit and allow us to attempt file repairs and configuration changes to non-working storage volumes.

The most commonly used file repair tool for hard drive issues is fsck.(File System ChecK) With this tool you can run file integrity checks, health checks and many other useful features. If you have a hard drive that you wish to scan with fsck then you will need to identify its mount point. To do this, we will use the df command:

df -h

This command will output the current mount points of your system in a human-readable format. Here is an example of the output:

```
Filesystem     Size  Used Avail Use% Mounted on
udev           3.8G     0 3.8G   0% /dev
tmpfs          784M   29M 755M   4% /run
/dev/sda1      218G   56G 151G  27% /
```

From this output, you can see that the primary drive (/dev/sda1) is mounted as the root drive (/). If you wanted more information about the hard drive, you can use the parted utility to view the partitions on it with the following:

parted /dev/sda1 'print'

Which outputs the following for my system:

```
Model: Unknown (unknown)
Disk /dev/sda1: 238GB
Sector size (logical/physical): 512B/512B
Partition Table: loop
Disk Flags:
Number  Start  End   Size   File system  Flags
1       0.00B  238GB 238GB  ext4
```

From this output, you can tell which number the hard drive is listed as, how much free space it has, and the format that the drive has been set up with. All of this information can help to identify problematic drives when you are having issues with your file system.

Useful Linux Commands for System Administrators
This is not complete but it's a compact list of commands to refer to when needed. Let us start one by one how we can use those commands with examples.

1. Uptime Command

In Linux **uptime command** shows how long your system is running and the number of users who are currently logged in and also displays the **load average of a system** for **1**, **5**, and **15** minutes intervals.

```
# uptime

08:16:26 up 22 min,  1 user,  load average: 0.00, 0.03,
0.22
```

Check Uptime Version

Uptime command don't have other options other than **uptime** and **version**. It gives information only in **hours:mins:sec** if it is less than **1** day.

```
# uptime -V
```

```
procps version 3.2.8
```

2. W Command

The **w command** will display <u>users currently logged in</u> and their process along with showing **load averages**, **login name**, **tty name**, **remote host**, **login time**, **idle time**, **JCPU**, **PCPU**, command, and processes.

```
# w

08:27:44 up 34 min,  1 user,  load average: 0.00, 0.00,
0.08
USER    TTY    FROM         LOGIN@  IDLE  JCPU
PCPU WHAT
tecmint  pts/0  192.168.50.1   07:59   0.00s 0.29s
0.09s w
```

Available Options

- **-h** : displays no header entries.
- **-s** : without JCPU and PCPU.
- **-f** : Removes from the field.
- **-V** : (upper letter) – Shows versions.

3. Users Command

Users command displays currently logged-in users. This command doesn't have other parameters other than help and version.

```
# users

tecmint
```

4. Who Command

who command simply returns the **user name**, **date**, **time,** and **host information**. who command is similar to **w** command. Unlike the **w** command **who** doesn't print what users are doing. Let's illustrate and see the difference between **who** and **w** commands.

```
# who

tecmint  pts/0    2012-09-18 07:59 (192.168.50.1)
# w

08:43:58 up 50 min,  1 user,  load average: 0.64, 0.18, 0.06
USER   TTY   FROM        LOGIN@  IDLE  JCPU PCPU WHAT
tecmint pts/0  192.168.50.1   07:59   0.00s 0.43s 0.10s w
```

Who command Options

- **-b**: Displays last system reboot date and time.
- **-r**: Shows current runlet.
- **-a, -all**: Displays all information cumulatively.

5. Whoami Command

In Linux, a **whoami** command is used to print the currently logged-in username into your Linux system. If you are logged in as a root using sudo command "**whoami**" command return **root** as the current user.

```
# whoami

tecmint
```

6. ls Command

ls command displays a list of files in a human-readable format.

```
# ls -l

total 114
dr-xr-xr-x.   2 root root  4096 Sep 18 08:46 bin
dr-xr-xr-x.   5 root root  1024 Sep  8 15:49 boot
```

Sort file as per last modified time.

```
# ls -ltr

total 40
-rw-r--r--. 1 root root  6546 Sep 17 18:42
install.log.syslog
-rw-r--r--. 1 root root 22435 Sep 17 18:45 install.log
```

```
-rw-------. 1 root root  1003 Sep 17 18:45 anaconda-
ks.cfg
```

7. Crontab Command

List schedule jobs for current user
with **crontab** command and -l option.

```
# crontab -l

00 10 * * * /bin/ls >/ls.txt
```

Edit your **crontab** with -e the option. In the below
example will open schedule jobs in **VI editor**. Make
necessary changes and quit pressing :wq keys that save
the setting automatically.

```
# crontab -e
```

8. Less Command

less command allows quickly viewing the file. You can
page up and down. Press 'q' to quit from less window.

```
# less install.log

Installing setup-2.8.14-10.el6.noarch
warning: setup-2.8.14-10.el6.noarch: Header V3
RSA/SHA256 Signature, key ID c105b9de: NOKEY
Installing filesystem-2.4.30-2.1.el6.i686
Installing ca-certificates-2010.63-3.el6.noarch
Installing xml-common-0.6.3-32.el6.noarch
```

```
Installing tzdata-2010l-1.el6.noarch
Installing iso-codes-3.16-2.el6.noarch
```

9. More Command

more command allows quickly view file and shows details in percentage. You can page up and down. Press 'q' to quit out from more window.

```
# more install.log

Installing setup-2.8.14-10.el6.noarch
warning: setup-2.8.14-10.el6.noarch: Header V3
RSA/SHA256 Signature, key ID c105b9de: NOKEY
Installing filesystem-2.4.30-2.1.el6.i686
Installing ca-certificates-2010.63-3.el6.noarch
Installing xml-common-0.6.3-32.el6.noarch
Installing tzdata-2010l-1.el6.noarch
Installing iso-codes-3.16-2.el6.noarch
--More--(10%)
```

10. CP Command

A **cp command** copies file from source to destination preserving the same mode.

```
# cp -p fileA fileB
```

You will be prompted before overwriting to file.

```
# cp -i fileA fileB
```

11. MV Command

An **mv command** renames **fileA** to **fileB** using the **-i** option, which prompts confirmation before overwriting. Ask for confirmation if exist already.

```
# mv -i fileA fileB
```

12. Cat Command

The **cat** command is used to view multiple files at the same time.

```
# cat fileA fileB
```

You combine **more** and **less** command with cat command to view file contain if that doesn't fit in single screen/page.

```
# cat install.log | less

# cat install.log | more
```

13. cd command (change directory)

with the **cd command** (change directory or switch directory) it will go to **fileA** directory.

```
# cd /fileA
```

14. pwd command (print working directory)

A **pwd command** return with the present working directory.

```
# pwd

/root
```

15. Sort command

The sort command is used to sort lines of text files in ascending order. with -r options will sort in descending order.

```
# sort fileA.txt

# sort -r fileA.txt
```

16. VI Command

Vi is the most popular text editor available in most **UNIX-like OS**. Below examples open file in read-only with -R option. Press ':q' to quit from vi windows.

```
# vi -R /etc/shadows
```

17. SSH Command (Secure Shell)

SSH command is used to login into the remote host. For example, the below ssh command will connect to the remote host (**192.168.50.2**) using the user as **Narad**.

```
# ssh narad@192.168.50.2
```

To check the version of ssh use the option -V (uppercase) shows version of ssh.

```
# ssh -V

OpenSSH_8.2p1 Ubuntu-4ubuntu0.3, OpenSSL 1.1.1f  31
Mar 2020
```

18. Ftp or sftp Command

ftp or <u>sftp</u> command is used to connect to remote ftp host. ftp is (**file transfer protocol**) and sftp is (**secure file transfer protocol**). For example, the below commands will connect to ftp host (**192.168.50.2**).

```
# ftp 192.168.50.2

# sftp 192.168.50.2
```

Putting multiple files in remote host
with **mput** similarly, we can do **mget** to download
multiple files from the remote host.

```
# ftp > mput *.txt

# ftp > mget *.txt
```

19. Systemctl Command

<u>Systemctl command</u> is a systemd management tool that is used to manage services, check running statuses, start and enable services and work with the configuration files.

```
# systemctl start httpd.service

# systemctl enable httpd.service

# systemctl status httpd.service
```

20. Free command

The **free command** shows **free, total,** and **swap memory** information in bytes.

```
# free
        total    used    free   shared  buffers   cached
Mem:    1030800  735944  294856      0    51648
547696
-/+ buffers/cache:   136600   894200
Swap:   2064376     0  2064376
```

Free with -t options show **total memory** used and available to use in bytes.

```
# free -t
        total    used    free   shared  buffers   cached
Mem:    1030800  736096  294704      0    51720
547704
-/+ buffers/cache:   136672   894128
Swap:   2064376     0  2064376
```

Total: 3095176   736096   2359080

21. Top Command

top command displays processor activity of your system and also displays tasks managed by kernel in real-time. It'll show **processor** and **memory** are being used. Using the top command with u the option will display specific User process details as shown below. Press 'O' (**uppercase letter**) to sort as desired by you. Press 'q' to quit from the top screen.

```
# top -u tecmint

top - 11:13:11 up  3:19,  2 users,  load average: 0.00,
0.00, 0.00
Tasks: 116 total,   1 running, 115 sleeping,   0 stopped,
0 zombie
Cpu(s):  0.0%us,  0.3%sy,  0.0%ni, 99.7%id,  0.0%wa,
0.0%hi,  0.0%si,  0.0%st
Mem:  1030800k total,   736188k used,   294612k free,
51760k buffers
Swap: 2064376k total,      0k used, 2064376k free,
547704k cached

PID USER    PR NI VIRT RES SHR S %CPU %MEM
TIME+  COMMAND
1889 tecmint  20   0 11468 1648  920 S 0.0  0.2
0:00.59 sshd
1890 tecmint  20   0 5124 1668 1416 S 0.0  0.2
0:00.44 bash
```

```
6698 tecmint   20   0 11600 1668  924 S  0.0  0.2
0:01.19 sshd
6699 tecmint   20   0  5124 1596 1352 S  0.0  0.2
0:00.11 bash
```

22. Tar Command

The **tar** command is used to compress files and folders in Linux. For example, the below command will create an archive for **/home** directory with the file name **archive-name.tar**.

```
# tar -cvf archive-name.tar /home
```

To extract the tar archive file use the option as follows.

```
# tar -xvf archive-name.tar
```

23. Grep Command

grep command search for a given string in a file. Only **tecmint** user displays from **/etc/passwd** file. we can use -i an option for ignoring case sensitivity.

```
# grep tecmint /etc/passwd

tecmint:x:500:500::/home/tecmint:/bin/bash
```

24. Find Command

Find command used to search **files, strings,** and **directories**. The below example of find command search **tecmint** word in '/' partition and return the output.

```
# find / -name tecmint

/var/spool/mail/tecmint
/home/tecmint
/root/home/tecmint
```

25. lsof Command

lsof mean List of all open files. Below lsof a command list of all opened files by user **tecmint**.

```
# lsof -u tecmint

COMMAND PID  USER FD TYPE   DEVICE SIZE/OFF
NODE NAME
sshd  1889 tecmint cwd  DIR    253,0  4096   2 /
sshd  1889 tecmint txt  REG    253,0 532336
298069 /usr/sbin/sshd
sshd  1889 tecmint DEL  REG    253,0      412940
/lib/libcom_err.so.2.1
sshd  1889 tecmint DEL  REG    253,0      393156
/lib/ld-2.12.so
sshd  1889 tecmint DEL  REG    253,0      298643
/usr/lib/libcrypto.so.1.0.0
sshd  1889 tecmint DEL  REG    253,0      393173
/lib/libnsl-2.12.so
sshd  1889 tecmint DEL  REG    253,0      412937
/lib/libkrb5support.so.0.1
```

```
sshd    1889 tecmint  DEL   REG    253,0        412961
/lib/libplc4.so
```

=

26. last command

With the last command, we can watch the user's activity
in the system. This command can execute normal users
also. It will display complete user's info
like **terminal**, **time**, **date**, **system**
reboot or **boot,** and **kernel version**. A useful command
to troubleshoot.

```
# last

tecmint  pts/1     192.168.50.1    Tue Sep 18 08:50
still logged in
tecmint  pts/0     192.168.50.1    Tue Sep 18 07:59
still logged in
reboot   system boot 2.6.32-279.el6.i Tue Sep 18 07:54 -
11:38  (03:43)
root    pts/1      192.168.50.1    Sun Sep 16 10:40 -
down   (03:53)
root    pts/0      :0.0         Sun Sep 16 10:36 - 13:09
(02:32)
root    tty1      :0          Sun Sep 16 10:07 - down
(04:26)
reboot   system boot 2.6.32-279.el6.i Sun Sep 16 09:57 -
14:33  (04:35)
narad   pts/2      192.168.50.1    Thu Sep 13 08:07 -
down   (01:15)
```

You can use **last** with **username** to know for specific user's activity as shown below.

```
# last tecmint

tecmint  pts/1      192.168.50.1    Tue Sep 18 08:50
still logged in
tecmint  pts/0      192.168.50.1    Tue Sep 18 07:59
still logged in
tecmint  pts/1      192.168.50.1    Thu Sep 13 08:07 -
down  (01:15)
tecmint  pts/4      192.168.50.1    Wed Sep 12 10:12 -
12:29  (02:17)
```

27. ps command

The ps command displays processes running in the system. The below example show the **init** to process only.

```
# ps -ef | grep init

root    1   0 0 07:53 ?      00:00:04 /sbin/init
root  7508 6825 0 11:48 pts/1   00:00:00 grep init
```

28. kill command

Use the kill command to terminate the process. First, find process **id** with **ps** command as shown below and kill the process with **kill -9** command.

```
# ps -ef | grep init
```

```
root      1    0  0 07:53 ?      00:00:04 /sbin/init
root     7508  6825  0 11:48 pts/1   00:00:00 grep init

# kill- 9 7508
```

29. rm command

rm command used to remove or delete a file without prompting for confirmation.

```
# rm filename
```

Use the **-i** option to get confirmation before removing it. Using options '**-r**' and '**-f**' will remove the file forcefully without confirmation.

```
# rm -i test.txt

rm: remove regular file `test.txt'?
```

30. mkdir command example.

mkdir command is used to create directories under Linux.

```
# mkdir directoryname
```

This is a handy day-to-day used basic commands in Linux / Unix-like operating system. Kindly share through our comment box if we missed out.

linux administartion glossary

Here are some common Linux administration terms and their definitions:

1. Kernel: The core component of the Linux operating system that manages hardware resources and provides basic services for other software.
2. Distribution (distro): A specific version of Linux that includes a particular set of software packages and configurations.
3. File system: The structure used by the operating system to organize and manage files on disk or other storage devices.
4. Command line interface (CLI): A method of interacting with the operating system using text commands entered into a terminal window.
5. Graphical user interface (GUI): A visual interface used to interact with the operating system and applications using windows, icons, and menus.
6. Package manager: A tool used to manage software packages, including installation, updates, and removal.
7. Service: A program or process that runs in the background and provides a specific function or functionality, such as a web server or database.
8. Shell: A command line interface that allows users to interact with the operating system and execute commands.

9. Cron: A tool used to schedule and automate recurring tasks or scripts.
10. SSH (Secure Shell): A protocol used to securely connect to a remote system and execute commands or transfer files.
11. Firewall: A security feature that controls network traffic to protect against unauthorized access or attacks.
12. RAID (Redundant Array of Independent Disks): A method of combining multiple hard drives into a single logical volume to improve performance, reliability, or both.
13. Virtualization: A technology that allows multiple virtual machines to run on a single physical machine, enabling better resource utilization and easier management.
14. SELinux (Security-Enhanced Linux): A security feature that provides mandatory access control to restrict access to system resources based on user roles and permissions.
15. Backup: The process of making a copy of data or files to protect against data loss or corruption.

www.ingramcontent.com/pod-product-compliance
Lightning Source LLC
Chambersburg PA
CBHW070917220526
45467CB00004B/1447